DREAMS AND THE DREAMWORLD

YOUR NAVIGATION COMPANION IN THE DREAM LAND

BY

ELSON ENOCH OWUSU SEKYERE

Unless otherwise, all scripture verses are taken from the American King James Bible.

For any inquiries, please contact the Author

Elson Enoch Owusu Sekyere

E-mail: thejourneyofaprophet@gmail.com

DEDICATION

Dedication

To the Dreamers—

To those who see beyond what is, who listen for whispers in the night, who treasure visions and dare to believe that God still speaks through dreams.

This book is for you—the ones who wake with wonder and wrestle with meaning, who journal faithfully and pray for understanding, who hold onto hope even when the vision tarries.

May your dreams become seeds of faith, planted in the soil of God's promises, and may you always know that the Giver of dreams is also the One who brings them to life.

Keep dreaming, keep seeking....

Table of Content

ACKNOWLEDGMENT

I extend my deepest gratitude to Almighty God, the source of all wisdom and inspiration, for entrusting me with this assignment and for guiding every step in the creation of this book. His divine inspiration and grace have made this work possible.

To my beloved family, I sincerely appreciate your unwavering love, patience, and support throughout this journey. Your encouragement has been a constant source of strength and motivation.

Lastly, I offer my heartfelt thanks to you, the readers, for embracing this message and participating in this Move. May this book inspire and empower you to grow in faith, purpose, and spiritual understanding.

ENDORSEMENT

Beloved, as we walk through the journey of life, we are often blessed with dreams, those divine whispers that connect us to realms unseen. Too many of us have dismissed these dreams, viewing them as mere flights of fancy or the workings of our subconscious. However, I believe that dreams are much more than that. They are sacred vessels through which God speaks to His children, inviting us into a deeper relationship with Him and offering wisdom for our lives.

In *Dreams and the Dream World:* Apostle Elson invites us to look beyond our limited understanding and recognize the profound power that dreams hold. This work reveals how dreams can be powerful messages from God, channels of divine revelation, and tools of spiritual growth. As we delve into the pages of this book, we are reminded that our dreams are not mere random thoughts; they are invitations from God Himself to guide, protect, and transform us.

The stories of Joseph, Daniel, and others from Scripture remind us that dreams are not just to be interpreted but to be acted upon. Through these biblical accounts, we learn that God's messages in dreams can shape our decisions, our paths, and even the course of nations. Dreams are a divine tool, given to us not just for reflection but for action.

What makes this book especially valuable is its focus on helping us navigate the dream world with discernment and responsibility. It equips us to recognize the different sources of our dreams—whether divine, soulish, or even demonic—and to protect our souls from the negative and harmful influences that may seek to infiltrate our minds as we sleep. This book calls us to take ownership of our spiritual lives, to guard our hearts and minds with integrity, and to sow seeds of faith that will bear fruit for the Kingdom of God.

I encourage you, dear reader, to embrace this work as an invitation to explore the divine language of dreams. As you do, may your understanding grow, and may your dreams become a powerful channel through which God speaks, offering you clarity, peace, and direction on your spiritual journey.

May your dreams not only reveal God's will but lead you closer to the fulfillment of your God-given purpose. May they be a source of divine revelation, a guide on your path, and a reminder of the depth of God's love and care for you.

Apostle Isaac W PNeuton
Christ Ambassadors Ministries. Int

FORWARD

The book, Dreams and the Dream World by Elson Enoch Owusu Sekyere is a must-read, especially to many in this generation who despise and disregard dreams and its implications in the physical realms. God, in His word, emphasises how He speaks to men through dreams. Dreams are, therefore, essential parts of our human existence. In the African Akan dialect from Ghana, which source from the hebrew language called dream 'dayɛ' ; 'da' for sleep and 'yɛ' for do, together to mean what one does when asleep. When the body is put to rest, the spirit is still active in the soulish and spirit realm from where we encounter secrets and warnings that help us in our day to day activities. This book is recommended not only for Christians but everybody because, irrespective of religion, you will dream. May it bless all that read in Jesus's name.

Prophet Kwadwo Agyemang
Overcomers Ministry Worldwide
Ghana - Ohwim, Kumasi

Chapter 1

The Burden of Love

"When the purpose of a thing is unknown, abuse is inevitable" - **Myles Munroe.**

I thank our Lord and Master Jesus Christ for the privilege and grace to understand and interpret dreams and the dream world. One of the chosen channels of God to speak to men, even when they are unskilled in hearing Him, is with Dreams.

Job 33:14-18 KJV

14 **For God speaks once, yes twice,** ***yet man perceives it not***.

15 In a dream, in a vision of the night, when deep sleep falls on men, in slumberings on the bed;

16 Then he opens the ears of men, and seals their instruction,

17 That he may withdraw man from his purpose, and hide pride from man.

18 He keeps back his soul from the pit, and his life from perishing by the sword.

Assuming that one does not regard their dreams with seriousness, or perhaps even trivializes, or lacks the spiritual knowledge to utilize them fully, it raises the question: How could God's intervention redirect one from a fruitless endeavor towards a more righteous path and shield one from pride? When pride is complete, you will certainly fall either into a pit or on a sword. Proverbs 16:18 Pride goeth before destruction, and a haughty spirit before a fall.

The benevolence and compassion of the divine are boundless, perpetually extending a hand to salvage humanity. Upon Adam's transgression, divine visitation occurred. Similarly, when sin was imminent for Cain, he also received a visit. Even in the face of regret for creating man, due to the persistent evil in the human imagination, divine communication was extended to Noah to prevent the total annihilation of humanity.

Genesis 6:5: *"And GOD saw that the wickedness of man was great in the earth, and that every imagination of the thoughts of his heart was only evil continually."*

What Greater love is this?

I write not these things to you from the place of abundance of information but as an extension of God's love that can preserve destinies through the revelation of dreams.

1 Corinthians 13:1 *If I have the gift of prophecy and can fathom all mysteries and* *all knowledge, and if I have a faith that can move mountains, **but have not love, I am nothing**.*

Accept this writing as a co-heir with you in Christ, extending the love of God and that you will also benefit from this grace.

In the capacity of an individual ceaselessly striving to comprehend the essence of our Lord Jesus, it is not my wish to witness the followers of God succumbing due to an absence of productive knowledge concerning dreams and the realm of dreams. Significant salvation and preservation can be imparted to the children of God once a comprehensive understanding of the dream world is attained.

By dreams, guidance on many inventions have touched the earth's realm, by a dream, the world was preserved when Joseph interpreted and acted upon the pharaoh's dream, and an evil that would have ravished a whole family was averted.

What a great gift God has prepared for both the skilled and unskilled. The righteous and even unrighteous whom he chooses to preserve. Shall a man abuse such great deliverance? Except he is uneducated in understanding dreams and the dream world.

A True Story : A Dream that Lead to Amputed Legs.

This lady immersed herself in a dream in the night's quiet solitude. The dream was vivid, almost too real, as if she was living another life. In this dream, she had an unfortunate encounter with a nail that pierced her left foot. Upon waking, she was startled to discover visible cracks in her toes, a surreal manifestation of her dream.

As days passed, the condition of her leg deteriorated rapidly. Three days later, it had reached a state of decay beyond any natural comprehension. With a heavy heart, she sought medical attention, hoping for a miracle. However, the prognosis was grim. The doctors, after a thorough examination, concluded that amputation was the only viable option to prevent further complications.

Two years after the life-altering surgery, she found herself in the throes of another dream. This time, her right leg was the victim of a sharp nail. The dream was eerily similar to the one she had before the amputation of her left leg. Upon waking, she was filled with a sense of dread, fearing the worst.

She rushed to the hospital, praying for a different outcome. However, the doctors were baffled by her condition. They suggested that her predicament was beyond medical science and recommended that she seek divine intervention. With no other options left, they proceeded with the amputation of her right leg.

The dreams, the accidents, and the subsequent amputations were a series of unfortunate events that seemed more than mere coincidences. They were mysterious and inexplicable, leaving her questioning the very fabric of reality. She couldn’t work to feed herself and her family any more.

This world is carpeted with evil, yet the Lord's provisions are great if we learn to adhere to him.

Dreams hold immense power, shaping our reality with both positive and negative outcomes. Enclosed is a comprehensive guide on dreams, crafted to equip you with the tools to confidently navigate their complexities, ensuring you can easily overcome any negative impacts they may have on your circumstances.

Yesterday is today's memory, and tomorrow is today's dream. If you can decode and seize your dreams today, tomorrow will be secure.

Chapter 2

The Dream World

The dream world is within us, transcending beyond the physical body but active mainly in the soul even convergence of the soul and the spirit. This very place is the imaginary plane. The imaginary plane holds the ability to form mental images or concepts that are not present in reality and can be a continuous and conscious mental process.

But the imaginary plane of the spiritualized mind is occupied not only by the owner of the soul but also by other spirits. It becomes a ground where instructions are sealed in the form of mental images in the soul of the man for perceiving, interpretation, and guidance.

The analogy of the dream world as a land gives illumination and a deeper understanding of how the dream world operates. The seeds you sow on it determine the predominant behavior of the nature of dreams and how you behave in your dreams.

Matthew 13:25-28a KJV

25 but while men slept, his enemy came and sowed tares among the wheat and went his way.

26 But when the grain had sprouted and produced a crop, then the tares also appeared.

27 So the servants of the owner came and said to him, 'Sir, did you not sow good seed in your field? How then does it have tares?'

28 He said to them, 'An enemy has done this.

You have to take responsibility for what is planted on this land else the destiny of your future dreams will be determined by it. The enemy always moves to and fro, looking for sleeping giants to plant tares amongst their wheat.

Man is the cultivator of his own soul. Whatever you sow in this, your soul shall reap accordingly.

Sources of Dreams

GOD

Job 33:14-18 KJV

14 For God speaks once, yes twice, *yet man perceives it not*.

15 In a dream, in a vision of the night, when deep sleep falls on men, in slumberings on the bed;

16 Then he opens the ears of men, and seals their instruction.

Aside from all the numerous mediums God uses to minister to his children. Dreams are one of the profound platforms God also uses to reveal whatever instruction He sealed in your heart while you fall into slumbering.

The Message of the Flood

"As we drew to the tail end of the year 2022, I found myself immersed in a vivid dream. In this dream, I was in a vehicle with my family, journeying towards Florida. As we traversed the road, a chilling sight unfolded before us - a demon spinning in a clockwise motion within the sea.

This demonic presence seemed to stir the waters into a frenzy, causing them to rise and wreak havoc on the surrounding environment. Cables were severed, vehicles were swept away, houses were destroyed, and the entire area was submerged under the floodwaters.

In the dream, I realized that I had traveled to this location to warn the inhabitants, who were members of my ministry. Upon awakening, I relayed the dream to the people in question. To our collective relief, when the events of the dream transpired in reality, no harm befell the members of my ministry. This experience served as a stark reminder of the power of dreams and the importance of heeding their warnings.

The Man's Soul

In a profound conversation, Jesus addressed Peter with a statement of deep spiritual significance. He said, "Peter, the revelation you have received is not of flesh and blood, but from my Father in heaven." This statement underscores the divine origin of Peter's understanding, emphasizing that it was not a product of human intellect or sensory perception but a divine revelation.

However, it is important to note that flesh and blood, our physical beings, are capable of revealing things. These could be experiences, perceptions, or insights often shaped by the cacophony of our lives - the noise, the character traits we exhibit, and the activities we engage in. These elements constitute the fabric of our soul, influencing our thoughts, actions, and dreams.

Yet, it is crucial to discern that not all dreams carry spiritual meanings. Many of them could be reflections of our own making, echoes of our daily lives, or manifestations of our minds. They may not necessarily hold spiritual significance or divine revelations.

This understanding invites us to navigate our spiritual journey with discernment, recognizing the difference between divine revelations and the echoes of our souls. It encourages us to seek the wisdom of the Lord and open our hearts to the word of the Lord that transcends our human understanding. Our imaginary plane holds the ability to form mental images or concepts that are not present in reality and can be a continuous and conscious mental process.

Ecclesiastes 5:3. The verse reads, "For a dream comes with much business and a fool's voice with many words"

Do you remember the analogy of your soul as a land? What you engage in the most becomes a seed planted on the land. While you are asleep, you gain the ability to see what is in your unconscious mind.

The Spiritual Merchant rightly said; man is a cultivator of his own soul.

A highly discerning individual possesses the ability to comprehend one's personality, mindset, and energy state merely by interpreting their dreams. The subconscious mind gathers information that one may not be fully aware of and subsequently replays it during sleep. This process reveals one's subconscious thoughts and feelings.

A typical case of dreams that a man's soul stirs in a good way is one I had in 2023; while in Texas with my family, we encountered a mechanical issue with our vehicle. The driver's side window was malfunctioning, and I took it upon myself to rectify the issue. Despite several hours of effort, the problem persisted, leading to a significant amount of frustration.

In need of a respite, I decided to rest and inadvertently fell asleep. During this period of rest, I dreamt of successfully repairing the window. Upon awakening, I approached the vehicle and applied the solution from my dream to the real-world problem. To my astonishment, my dream resolved the issue with the window. This experience served as a testament to the power of Dream Solutions.

Evil spirits

Evil spirits have a way of transmitting information into your dreams, either by controlling what happens around you or by visitations and visions. In the account of Luke chapter 4, we see satan showing Jesus visions while He fasted and prayed for 40 days and 40 nights. He shows Jesus the glories of this world **in a moment**.

Luke 4:5 Then the devil, taking Him up on a high mountain, showed Him all the kingdoms of the world in **a moment of time (A short period)**.

All these happened in the thought realm. Have you not heard that the weapons of our warfare are not of the flesh but mighty before God to the casting down of strongholds, **casting down imaginations**, and every high thing that is exalted against the knowledge of

God, and <u>bringing every thought into captivity</u> to the obedience of Christ;

Some enemies' attacks are targeted at your imaginary plane, which can heavily influence your dreams.

We saw how the devil showed Jesus all the kingdoms in a moment of time. This can't be a physical showing. It must certainly be a vision. Jesus could not travel to all the kingdoms of this world by flesh in just a moment of time. This can only be done by the instrumentation of a spiritual vehicle called a vision. But if such thing happens while you are asleep it is called the visions of the night.

This understanding awakens a great deal of responsibility to be intentional about how you relate with these channels (God, the devil and your soul) to successfully have dominion over the dream world.

The Devil's Deal

"Three years subsequent to my acceptance of Christ Jesus, I found myself immersed in a profound dream. In this dream, I was in an unfamiliar place, and I noticed a remarkable transformation - my teeth had metamorphosed into diamonds.

A woman appeared in the dream, expressing her interest in me. However, as the dream progressed, she underwent a startling transformation, morphing into an octopus in the midst of the sea. She began to promise me worldly possessions - fame, wealth, and luxury.

In the dream, I spotted a bottle of water. With a firm belief in my faith, I declared, 'I turn this water into the blood of Jesus.' As I consumed the water, the diamond teeth dislodged from my mouth.

Suddenly, the sea began to churn, and many creatures emerged, launching an attack. I found myself in the throes of a fierce battle, fighting back against the onslaught. At this point, I awoke from the dream, left to ponder its spiritual impression."

Gates and Passages into the dream world.

There are ignitions, or gates that create the environment of your dreams and the dream world. These ignitions can even affect the nature of the dreams that even God and the devil try to plant in your soul and imaginary plane. The gates are to be guarded with all diligence if you want to have flawless insight into your soul, God's and the devil's dreams.

I will teach you how to use the devil's dreams to your advantage in advance lessons. Joseph said in Genesis 50:20 (NKJV) But as for you, you meant evil against me; but God meant it for good, in order to bring it about as it is this day, to save many people alive. The act of turning evil arrows into good ones is an act of God. But in this book session, I will focus mainly on guarding the gates and ignitions that grant you passage into the purest dream world to facilitate the purposes of God through the dreams He gives you.

The Thought Gate: Your predominate thought can generate soulish dreams and invite demonic and divine dreams as well. Soulish dreams may reveal hidden personalities and predominant ones.

You would want to be cautious about your social media use and the movies you watch immediately before sleep. Since they are your immediate thoughts, you will likely carry them into your journey into the dream world.

The Gate of Desire: Your Desire is never ordinary. They are stronger voices that determine what your future will look like. Both God and the devil use it for and against man.

Philippians 2:13 for it is God who is at "work" in you, both to **desire** and to **work** for *His* good pleasure. (NASB).

The Meaning of the underlined word "work" is energéō means to "engaged in," properly energize. Desire then becomes the impartation of God's kind of energy to desire and to work for His good pleasure.

Likewise, the devil, James 1:14 But each one is tempted when he is drawn away by his **own desires** and enticed.

The devil has no grounds if you don't harbor sinful desires. When you do, then he draws you way into temptation. This also applies to the dream world.

"Your desires are loudspeakers calling upon the appearance of spirits into your life and dreams."

The Gate of Things: Sensory interactions with your environment can also play major roles in your dreams. There are little things that can hold spiritual influence in them for a long time; some inanimate objects have a memory they can pass on to you.

Acts 19:11-12 KJV God did extraordinary miracles through the hands of Paul,

so that **even handkerchiefs** and **aprons** <u>that had touched him</u> were taken to the sick, and the diseases and evil spirits left them.

These handkerchiefs and aprons that had touched Paul left him with a spiritual substance that could change the destiny of men. The sick was no more sick, and if those evil spirits were demons of poverty, then these people would become rich through an apron that touched God's servant. That particular individual came into contact with the right material qualified by the power of GOD through Paul. What if Paul was a sorcerer? Who slept in the bed of the same hotel room you are lodging in? What dreams do you think you will have?

Territorial Gates: Some locations are positively or negatively charged spiritually. You are likely to get a spiritual experience at a high rate. Jacob when he got to the exact location where Abraham, his grandfather, built an altar and a covenant with the Lord. He laid on a stone to sleep. I don’t think using a stone as a pillow is comfortable. But that night, he had a dream affirming his father's covenant with God. Ask yourself. Why that location, and why a stone as a pillow? **His testimony was God was here, and I didn't know.**

Genesis 28:11-22 NKJV

11 So he came to a certain place and stayed there all night because the sun had set. And <u>he took one of the stones</u> of that place and put it at his head, and he lay down in that place to sleep.

12 ***Then he dreamed****, and behold, a ladder was set up on the earth, and its top reached* to heaven, and there the angels of God were ascending and descending on it.

The Gate of Your Emotions

Sadness and ill thoughts, offense and lust, can stir up dreams in a man and can also make you receptive to dreams from spiritual entities. Imagine a scenario where you've had a minor disagreement with your neighbor. The conflict has left you harboring ill-will, to the point where you find yourself wishing misfortune upon them. Suddenly, in the theater of your dreams, you witness something terrible befalling them.

Upon awakening, you experience a sense of satisfaction, believing your perceived adversary has been vanquished. However, it's crucial to understand that this is merely a dream, a creation of your own mind, fueled by your current emotions and not a reflection of reality.

Your neighbor is not your enemy. Disagreements and conflicts are part of human interaction, but they do not define the entirety of a relationship. It's essential to approach such situations with the spirit of reconciliation, embodying the teachings of Christ, who advocated love and forgiveness.

As followers of Christ, we are reminded of his words to his disciples, emphasizing the importance of love and forgiveness over vengeance. We are not bearers of the spirit of Elisha, who called down a curse, but of Christ, who taught us to turn the other cheek.

This understanding can guide us in our interactions, helping us to see beyond temporary conflicts and fostering a spirit of neighborliness and mutual respect.

The Hour of dreams – Time zones and dreams.

Job 33:15-18 KJV In a dream, *in a vision of the night*, When deep sleep falleth upon men, In slumberings upon the bed; Then he openeth the ears of men, And sealeth their instruction

Genesis 1:5 God called the light "day," and the darkness He called "night." And there was evening, and there was morning— the first day.

God can speak to His people in dreams whenever they sleep. In the personal dealing of specific people, God could provide them with an hour of dreams (a time when they have to be on their bed to receive messages from the Lord). This is not the general rule, but if you find out that your dreams consistently fall on specific times over the years, God may be speaking to you to pay attention to that time.

What if I travel to a location with a different time zone?

God called day and night. That is what he created. The clock is a human interpretation of what God created for a universal language. So, time zones don't change the time of your dream encounters if you have one.

Chapter 3

Special Forms of Dreams

The significance of dreams tends to amplify when they adopt specific forms. In this discussion, we will concentrate on several forms and their respective implications, namely nested dreams and recurring dreams.

Nested Dreams

This phenomenon refers to the occurrence of a dream within another dream, a state where one is dreaming while already in a dream. This type of dream carries profound significance and often conveys a profound message from the divine. Typically, the inner dream encapsulates the central message being conveyed by the divine, while the outer dream serves to reinforce or validate the message of the inner dream.

Recurring dreams

Recurring dreams are different and not the same as dream duplication, where the dream repeats itself just twice. A typical case is the dream of Pharoah (Gen 41), which has the same message but different storylines on the same night.

Recurring dreams are when the dreams keep repeating themselves repeatedly and you don't know why you keep having the same dream.

When you keep on having repeated dreams, it tends to point to a problem or an issue in the dreamer's life, and the Lord is trying to get the dreamer to address this issue in their life, but the dreamer is not getting it, that's why the dream keeps repeating so that you can get the message the Lord is relating in the dream.

The Three types of recurring dreams

Periodic Recurring Dreams

This refers to the experience of having a recurring dream within the same week, month, or year. Upon awakening, you are left with a sense of unease and a feeling of elusive understanding regarding the dream's content.

You may have a recurring dream throughout the year where you're climbing a mountain but never reach the top. Each time you wake up, you're left with a feeling of incompleteness and a nagging sensation that there's a deeper message within the dream that you can't quite grasp.

Another typical case could be a dream about an old friend you haven't spoken to in years. The dream leaves you feeling unsettled and curious, as you can't pinpoint why this person suddenly appeared in your dreams. This happens in the same week.

Scheduled Recurring Dream

This type comes in a specific schedule, and it comes the same day each month, the same day each year or the same month each year; examples that illustrate the type of dreams that adhere to a specific schedule, recurring on the same day each month, the same day each year, or the same month each year. It could be every year on your birthday, and you have a dream about childhood classmates with you paying admission fees. This dream recurs annually on the same day.

Another could be you have a dream on the 15th of every month where you're walking along a cemetery. The dream is consistent and occurs without fail on the same day each month.

Also, it could be that you always, without fail get sexual dreams every afternoon.

Fraternal Recurring Dream

This type of dream has the same message but a different storyline, an example is Pharaoh's dream.

Genesis chapter 41

1 Then it came to pass, at the end of two full years, that Pharaoh had a dream; and behold,
he stood by the river. 2 Suddenly there came up out of the river seven cows, fine looking
and fat; and they fed in the meadow. 3 Then
behold, seven other cows came up after them

out of the river, ugly and gaunt, and stood by
the other cows on the bank of the river. 4 And
the ugly and gaunt cows ate up the seven fine
looking and fat cows. So, Pharaoh awoke. 5
He slept and dreamed a second time; and
suddenly seven heads of grain came up on
one stalk, plump and good. 6 Then behold,
seven thin heads, blighted by the east wind,
sprang up after them. 7 And the seven thin
heads devoured the seven plump and full
heads. So, Pharaoh awoke, and indeed, it was
a dream. 8 Now it came to pass in the
morning that his spirit was troubled, and he
sent and called for all the magicians of Egypt
and all its wise men. And Pharaoh told them
his dreams, but there was no one who could
interpret them for Pharaoh.

Live Coverage Dreams

Live Coverage Dreams are a profound phenomenon where God sends immediate answers to real-life issues, offering clarity and direction. These prophetic dreams deliver inspired solutions, heavenly guidance, and spiritual epiphanies, helping individuals navigate life's challenges with confidence and wisdom. One can tap into supernatural guidance by paying attention to these dreams, unlocking hidden potential and fostering personal growth.

Live Coverage Dreams enhance decision-making skills, provide insight into complex problems, discover innovative solutions, and develop a deeper understanding of oneself and others.

By embracing these dreams, one can transform one's life, make informed decisions and navigate life's journey with purpose and conviction. Live Coverage dreams serve as a powerful tool, bridging the gap where natural solutions fail.

Joseph's Live Coverage Dreams

In the biblical account of Jesus' birth, Joseph, the earthly father of Jesus, received a series of Live coverage dreams that played a crucial role in the fulfilment of God's plan. These dreams served as a direct communication from God, providing Joseph with guidance, direction, and reassurance during a critical period in his life.

The First Dream: A Message of Reassurance

In Matthew 1:20-25, Joseph received his first dream, in which an angel appeared to him, saying, "Joseph, son of David, do not be afraid to take Mary home as your wife, because what is conceived in her is from the Holy Spirit." This dream reassured Joseph that Mary's pregnancy was indeed a divine miracle, and he should not hesitate to accept her as his wife. There was a real problem at hand and a crucial decision for Joseph to make. If the angel had not intervened, he would have stepped out of God's divine plan for his life. Live coverage dreams are God's interventions to keep you in His will.

The Second Dream: Divine Protection

In Matthew 2:13-15, Joseph received another dream, warning him of the danger that Jesus faced from King Herod. The angel instructed Joseph to flee to Egypt with Mary and Jesus, which they promptly did. This dream saved the life of Jesus, as Herod's plan was to kill all male children in Bethlehem. A live coverage dream preserved the life and destiny of Jesus. If God didn't hesitate to intervene in the life of Jesus, then we all must embrace and be aware of the necessity of taking the necessary action when heaven prompts us through live coverage dreams.

The Third Dream: Prophetic Alignment

In Matthew 2:19-23, Joseph received a third dream, in which the angel told him it was safe to return to Israel, as those seeking Jesus' life were dead. However, upon learning that Archelaus, Herod's son, was ruling in Judea, Joseph decided to settle in Nazareth instead, fulfilling another prophecy. We can see how God keeps using Live coverage dreams to watch over the life of Jesus, even to be aligned with prophecy. The prophecy in Isaiah 9:1-2, which mentions Galilee, is fulfilled in Jesus' ministry. Jesus' presence in Galilee brings light to a region that was previously in darkness.

These dreams were explicitly stated to be from God or His angels, providing specific instructions and direction for Joseph's actions. They occurred at critical moments, ensuring the protection and well-being of

Jesus and His family. Joseph's response to these dreams demonstrated his faith and willingness to obey God's guidance.

May the experience of live coverage dreams be activated in your life so you receive God's direct communication, providing guidance, protection, and direction in times of need.

When God Visited Abimelech in a Dream

In Genesis 20:3-7, we find an extraordinary account of God visiting Abimelech, the king of Gerar, in a dream. This live coverage dream served as a direct communication from God, conveying a critical message to Abimelech regarding his actions.

The Dream: A Divine Warning

God appeared to Abimelech in a dream, warning him that he was as good as dead because he had taken Sarah, Abraham's wife, into his harem. God's message was clear: Abimelech's actions had put him in danger of divine judgment.

The dream was explicitly stated to be from God providing a direct warning and instruction for Abimelech's actions.

- The dream conveyed the seriousness of Abimelech's situation, emphasizing the potential consequences of his actions and God addressed Abimelech directly, making it clear that He was speaking to him personally.

Abimelech promptly returned Sarah to Abraham, acknowledging God's authority and warning, acknowledging God's power and control over his life and kingdom.

Significance of the Dream

This live coverage dreams highlights:

God's direct communication: God communicates directly with individuals, regardless of their background or status.

God's concern for righteousness: God intervenes to protect the righteous (Abraham and Sarah) and warn the unrighteous (Abimelech).

The importance of obedience: Abimelech's prompt obedience to God's warning demonstrates the importance of responding to live coverage.

In this remarkable account, we see God using a dream to guide Abimelech, illustrating the power and significance of live coverage dreams in conveying divine direction and warning.

Prophetic dreams

Prophetic dreams are a powerful means of communication from God, revealing insights into past, present, and future events. These dreams are a vital part of the prophetic ministry, allowing individuals to receive guidance, wisdom, and revelation from the Lord.

Characteristics of Prophetic Dreams

1. Revelatory: Prophetic dreams reveal hidden truths, uncovering secrets and mysteries that are not yet known.

2. Informative: These dreams inform individuals about past, present, and future events, providing insight into the plans and purposes of God.

3. Symbolic: Prophetic dreams often use symbolism, metaphors, and allegories to convey messages, requiring interpretation and discernment.

4. Spiritual: These dreams operate on a spiritual level, transcending the natural realm and accessing the realm of the spirit.

Types of Prophetic Dreams

1. Warning Dreams: These dreams serve as warnings, alerting individuals to potential dangers, pitfalls, or challenges.

2. Instructional Dreams: These dreams provide guidance and instruction, offering wisdom and insight into specific situations or circumstances.

3. Revelatory Dreams: These dreams reveal hidden truths, uncovering secrets and mysteries that are not yet known.

4. Prophetic Declaration Dreams: These dreams declare the plans and purposes of God, announcing future events and outcomes.

Chapter 4

Dream Language

Dreams possess a universal language, yet they also contain symbols and tokens shaped by the dreamer's experiences. This is why dream dictionaries sometimes fall short in their interpretations. For instance, when Isaiah saw what we would now recognize as an airplane, he described it as "those who fly like a cloud, and like doves to their windows" because in his era, airplanes did not exist, and he used the symbol of doves for his description.

Your experiences and environment also influence the symbols in your dreams. For example, devout Christians who see a dove in their dreams may interpret it as the Holy

Spirit. However, if God were to show you Isaiah's vision, using modern dream interpretation dictionaries could lead to incorrect interpretations.

Nevertheless, there are eternal symbols that transcend generations. These symbols are highly accurate in their interpretations because they are not bound by time. For instance, if God wants to show you soldiers, you are likely to see them in the uniform of your nation's military rather than as the warriors of David's time.

The eternal language of God and the language of your generation or culture often shape the form of your dreams. We will delve deeper into this topic when we discuss the interpretation of dreams.

Chapter 5

THE LIFESTYLE OF DREAMER

"Dreamers are a unique breed of individuals who see beyond the present moment and envision a future through dreams. Because their mind is a receptacle, they should be conscious of how they live their lives and what they feed their mind to become vessels who receive and deliver pure streams of messages given to them in their dreams.

Zechariah 4: (AKJV)

"And I answered again, and said unto him, What be these two olive branches which through the two golden pipes empty the golden oil out of themselves?" [1 2]

They must be like the golden pipes that empty golden oil. On condition that the pipes are clogged, the oil will fail to flow; and if they are dirty, the golden oil will be tainted. Hence, it is a great responsibility to keep your vessel pure, O blessed dreamer."

"When Peter was shown a vision, his cultural background and personal beliefs invaded the vision and the instruction the Lord was asking him to adhere to. He told the Lord, 'Not so, Lord; for I have never eaten anything that is common or unclean. And the voice spoke to him again a second time, 'What God has cleansed, that call not thou common.'

According to the lifestyle and culture of his days, these animals were considered unclean, and that decision greatly impacted how he responded to the Lord's instruction." The lifestyle of a dreamer has a direct impact on his dreams; it is important to understand how successful dreamers in the bible lived and learn from their example.

"*For whatsoever things were written aforetime were written for our learning, that we through patience and comfort of the scriptures might have hope.*" Romans 15:4 (AKJV)

The Lifestyle of Integrity

Joseph, the earthly father of Jesus

In a world filled with deceit and dishonesty, a just man stands out as a beacon of hope and righteousness. Joseph, the earthly father of Jesus, is an exemplary model of integrity. As a just man, Joseph demonstrated unwavering honesty and principle-centered living, even in the face of adversity.

When Mary, his betrothed, was found to be with child, Joseph could have chosen to publicly shame her and divorce her. Instead, he chose to obey God's command and take Mary as his wife, raising Jesus as his own son (Matthew 1:18-19). This selfless act showcases Joseph's integrity, as he prioritized doing what was right over personal gain or reputation.

Abimelech, the king of Gerar

In Genesis 20:3-7, Abimelech, the king of Gerar, demonstrates remarkable integrity in his dealings with Abraham and God. When God appeared to Abimelech in a dream, revealing that Sarah, Abraham's wife, was actually his sister, Abimelech immediately took action.

(Genesis 20:3-4): "But God came to Abimelech in a dream by night, and said to him, Behold, thou art but a dead man, for the woman which thou hast taken; for she is a man's wife. But Abimelech had not come near her: and **he said, Lord, wilt thou slay also a righteous nation?"**

Abimelech was a righteous man and God's affirmation makes it remarkably true verse 6 "And God said unto him in a dream, Yea, I know that thou didst this in the integrity of thy heart; for I also withheld thee from sinning against me: therefore, suffered I thee not to touch her."

Abimelech said the integrity of my heart and innocence of my hands have I done this. And indeed, he refusing to take advantage of Sarah despite being King was nobel.

Joseph on of Jacob

(Genesis 39:7-10):

And it came to pass after these things, that his master's wife cast her eyes upon Joseph; and she said, Lie with me. But he refused and said unto his master's wife, Behold, my master wotteth not what is with me in the house, and he hath committed all that he hath to my hand; There is none greater in this house than I; neither hath he kept back anything from me but thee, because thou art his wife: **how then can I do this great wickedness, and sin against God**?"

Joseph's resistance to temptation and his honesty and integrity in the face of false accusations were among the key signs that he was a just man. These great dreamers benefited greatly because of their just lives, and in their dreams, we see that the Lord was with them. A just life draws the Lord to you, and He will speak and reveal His covenant to you (Psalm 25:14, AKJV).

As we studied earlier, "For a dream comes with a multitude of business, and a fool's voice with a multitude of words" (Ecclesiastes 5:3). Imagine if you are an unjust man - your dreams will be filled with it."

The Lifestyle of forgiveness

Unforgiveness is a toxic emotion that can consume our minds, hearts, souls therefore affecting our dreams. When we harbor unforgiveness, it can lead to a range of negative consequences like emotional pain, which can manifest as anger, resentment, bitterness, and hurt. (Proverbs 26:2; Matthew 6:14-15), including impacting our dreams.

Effects of Unforgiveness on Your Dreams

Inaccurate perception

The realm of dreams is not immune to the corrosive effects of unforgiveness. Just as in our waking hours, unforgiveness can significantly distort our perceptions and thought processes within the dreamscape, creating a nocturnal world viewed through a warped lens.

In dreams, our biased thinking manifests in surreal and often unsettling ways. Dreamscapes become populated with exaggerated villains and scenarios of betrayal, as our minds fixate on hurtful aspects of past situations while positive elements fade into the background. The dream world becomes a theater for our assumptions, where we expect the worst from others, their dream-selves acting out our darkest interpretations of their intentions.

The projection takes on a literal form in dreams, as we may find ourselves confronting shadowy figures who embody the very qualities, we refuse to acknowledge in ourselves. These dream encounters serve as stark reminders of the negative attributes we unknowingly attribute to those who have wronged us.

Emotions in dreams, already intense, become even more volatile under the influence of unforgiveness. Dream scenarios evoke exaggerated reactions, and the emotions of other dream figures are consistently misread, creating a landscape of perpetual misunderstanding and conflict. Our self-image in dreams may become distorted, manifesting as recurring themes of inadequacy, shame, or self-blame.

The dreamworld's fluid reality becomes even more unreliable as unforgiveness skews our interpretation of dream events. We draw incorrect conclusions from dream scenarios, further reinforcing our waking biases. Our dreaming mind struggles to empathize with other figures in our dreams, rendering their actions and motivations incomprehensible and often threatening.

Inverted dreams

The eye itself sees things in an inverted manner. When the brain processes these signals, it corrects the inversion and reversal, allowing us to see the world right-side up and forward. If this process fails, you begin to see things upside down. Likewise, when there is much unforgiveness in your soul, it creates bizarre and unsettling scenarios in which contradictory elements coexist. For example, you might see a man dying, but in reality, it was a woman; due to unforgiveness in your spirit, your perception turns things upside down. Spiritually, our dreams may become barren landscapes devoid of divine presence, mirroring the narrowing effect unforgiveness has on our spiritual understanding. In this way, the world of dreams becomes both a reflection and an amplification of the distortions caused by unforgiveness.

The Devil's Strength in Battle

Bitterness can become a legal weapon against you in the spirit, giving Satan a foothold in your life and hindering your spiritual growth. Consider the following consequences:

Gives Satan a foothold: Bitterness provides an entry point for Satan to attack and influence your life.

2 Corinthians 2:10-11

10 Anyone you forgive, I also forgive. And what I have forgiven—if there was anything to forgive—I have forgiven in the sight of Christ for your sake,

11 **in order that Satan might not outwit us. For we are not unaware of his schemes.**

Bitterness can hinder God's blessings and favor in your life (Psalm 66:18; Proverbs 10:22).

Bitterness can draw demonic entities, exacerbating spiritual struggles even to the extent of hindering the power of your prayers and connection with God.

Mark 11:25

And when you stand praying, if you hold anything against anyone, forgive them, so that your Father in heaven may forgive you your sins.

Bitterness can create cycles of pain and hurt, making it challenging to break free.

Breaking Free from Unforgiveness:

1. Acknowledge and Accept: Recognize the hurt and accept the emotions.

2. Let Go: Release the need for revenge, resentment, and anger. (Matthew 6:14-15; Luke 6:27-31)

3. Forgive: Choose to forgive, not for the other person's sake, but for yours. (Matthew 6:12; Mark

11:25)

4. Seek Healing: Pursue spiritual guidance, counseling, or therapy to address underlying issues.

(Proverbs 11:14; 2 Corinthians 1:3-4)

Chapter 6

Integrating Dream Insights into Daily Life

Receiving a dream from God is a precious gift, offering guidance, wisdom, and insight into His plans and purposes. However, simply receiving a dream is not enough; taking action on the revelation received is crucial.

The Importance of Acting on Divine Dreams

1. Obedience: Acting on a divine dream demonstrates obedience to God's will and instructions. It shows that you trust and value His guidance.

2. Faith: Taking action on a dream requires faith, trusting that God will provide the necessary resources, wisdom, and strength to accomplish the task.

3. Personal Growth: Acting on a divine dream can lead to significant personal growth, as you step out of your comfort zone and develop new skills and abilities.

4. Fulfillment of Purpose: By taking action on a divine dream, you can fulfill your God-given purpose and make a meaningful impact in the world.

The Consequences of Not Acting on Divine Dreams

1. Stagnation: Failing to act on a divine dream can lead to stagnation, causing you to miss out on opportunities for growth and development.

2. Disobedience: Ignoring a divine dream can be considered disobedience, potentially leading to a breakdown in your relationship with God.

3. Missed Opportunities: Not acting on a divine dream can result in missed opportunities, causing you to wonder what could have been accomplished if you had taken action.

4. Regret: Failing to act on a divine dream can lead to regret as you reflect on the possibilities that were not pursued.

How to practically Deal with Dreams.

Prayer

Praying over dreams is essential for manifesting positive visions and thwarting negative influences in your life.

It helps you align with God's will, allowing you to clarify and confirm the dream's alignment with His purposes. Through prayer, we gain insight into God's perspective on the dream, enabling us to see it from His viewpoint.

Additionally, prayer aids in overcoming obstacles and challenges. Many people treat such dreams casually, simply saying, "I cancel it" and assuming it is canceled. The worst are those who ignore the dreams entirely, thinking they won't manifest. Positive dreams require much prayer to come to fruition, while negative ones can manifest even without prayer. Until the Holy Spirit gives you an inner witness, don’t stop.

Prayer helps to break down barriers and obstacles that may hinder the fulfillment of the dream and also receive strength and courage to overcome challenges and persevere in the face of adversity.

Prayer provides strategic guidance on how to pursue the dream, including the steps to take and the decisions to make. There is an impartation of wisdom and discernment to navigate the journey and make wise choices.

Receiving a divine dream is a precious gift but only the beginning. Taking action on the revelation received is crucial, as it demonstrates obedience, faith, and a willingness to grow and fulfill your purpose. Remember, the consequences of not acting on a divine dream can be significant, leading to stagnation, disobedience, missed opportunities, and regret.

Sacrificially Giving

Isaiah 58:6-8

Is this not the fast that I have chosen? to loose the bonds of wickedness,To undo the heavy burdens,To let the oppressed go free,And that you break every yoke?

Is it not to share your bread with the hungry,

And that you bring to your house the poor who are cast out; When you see the naked, that you cover him, And not hide yourself from your own flesh?Then your light shall break forth like the morning,

Your **HEALING** shall spring forth speedily,And your righteousness shall go before you;**The glory of the LORD shall be your rear GUARD.**

This kind of fasting and giving causes you healing to spring forth speedily.

In Gods consistent character you see him even turn against Israel when their enemy sacrificed his only and first son. God loves a liberal soul.

Psalm 41:1-2: "Blessed is the one who considers the poor! In the day of trouble, the Lord delivers him; **the Lord protects him and keeps him alive; he is called blessed** in the land; <u>you do not give him up to the will of his enemies</u>.

How to Grow in Your Interpretation level of Dream

To develop greater skill in interpreting dreams, it is essential to recognize that true interpretation comes from God. God may choose to reveal interpretation insight to an individual through another dream, or He may endow a person with a unique spiritual gift for dream interpretation

Genesis 41:15-16:

15 Pharaoh said to Joseph, "I had a dream, and no one can interpret it. But I have heard it said of you that when you hear a dream you can interpret it."

16 Joseph answered Pharaoh, "It is not in me; God will give Pharaoh a favorable answer..'"

Pray to Receive interpretation of Dreams.

"He urged them to plead for mercy from the God of heaven concerning this mystery, so that he and his friends might not be executed with the rest of the wise men of Babylon. Daniel 2:18.

This was a collective prayer that led to God revealing the dream and its interpretation to Daniel in a vision later that night.

Daniel 2:19: "Then the mystery was revealed to Daniel in a vision of the night. Then Daniel blessed the God of heaven."

Pray for the Special Ability to Interpret dreams

Daniel 5:12: Daniel was given "an extraordinary spirit, knowledge and insight, **interpretation of dreams**, explanation of enigmas, and solving of difficult problems."

Key Word: Daniel was **GIVEN.** Taking time to ask God for the ability to interpret dreams is also a medium that God may use.

Honoring those who have that ability

This could be via gifts, seeds, service or holy reverence of what God is doing in a man life. This can also cause you to receive the ability to interpret dreams.

"He that receiveth a prophet in the name of a prophet shall receive a prophet's reward; and he that receiveth a righteous man in the name of a righteous man shall receive a righteous man's reward. And whosoever shall give to drink unto one of these little ones a cup of cold water only in the name of a disciple, verily I say unto you, he shall in no wise lose his reward. Matthew 10:41–42.

Journaling

The bible does provide examples and principles that support the value of recording God-given dreams. Throughout Scripture, significant dreams and their interpretations are carefully documented. For example, the dreams of Joseph (Genesis 37:5-11), Pharaoh (Genesis 41), and Nebuchadnezzar (Daniel 2, 4) are all recorded in detail, along with their outcomes and spiritual significance. This biblical pattern demonstrates that recording dreams preserves their meaning, allows for reflection, and helps track God's guidance over time.

Writing down dreams can aid in discernment, prayer, and interpretation, aligning with the biblical encouragement to remember and meditate on God's works (Psalm 77:11-12, Habakkuk 2:2). By journaling dreams, believers create a record that can be revisited

for greater understanding and to recognize patterns in how God speaks, which supports spiritual growth in interpreting dreams.

Dedicating 10-15 minutes each morning to remembering and reflecting on dreams. During this time, it is also a good practice to write down your vision for the night

You can document your dreams digitally, securing them with a password, or write them down manually—whichever method you prefer.

Seek Wise Counsel and Confirmation

Share significant or confusing dreams with pastor or anyone that as Dreams and interpretation as part of their main assignment with track record. Remember you don't want share your dreams with people because the pose to be spiritual.

Submitting dreams to verified ministers helps guard against misinterpretation and provides accountability.

Grow in Humility and Obedience

Approach dream interpretation with humility, recognizing that full understanding may not always come immediately. When a dream's meaning is clear and confirmed, act in obedience to God's guidance

Gratitude, Review and Reflect Regularly

Periodically revisit your dream journal to reflect on past dreams and their outcomes.

Thank God for His communication and note how your understanding of dreams grows over time.

RESOURCES

Munroe, M. (1992). Understanding the purpose and power of purpose (p. 13). Whitaker House.

Made in the USA
Columbia, SC
19 June 2025

59459554R00052